Contents

Above: Colourful lotus flowers grow in many wetlands in Borneo.

Top: Iban tribesman using a blowpipe and adorned with a colourful headdress made from Argus Pheasant tail feathers.

Above left: The richly decorated Puu Jih Shih Buddhist Temple in Sandakan, Sabah.

Chapter 1: Richness and Diversity

Few islands in the world evoke the sense of mystery and fascination that Borneo does. Throughout history, the world's third largest island (after Greenland and New Guinea, and excluding the continent of Australia) has attracted a rich array of merchants, adventurers and entrepreneurs, and now intrepid travellers and tourists can be added to the list of visitors as they pursue their own personal adventures in Borneo.

Below: Beaches and islands are popular with holidaymakers.

Bottom: Early morning mist above the tropical rainforest.

Three nations share the 743,330-km² (287,022-sq mile) island. Indonesian Kalimantan covers 73 per cent of it, the small, oil-rich sultanate of Brunei stakes a claim to a small area on the northwest coast and the Malaysian states of Sabah and Sarawak make up the rest. The East Malaysian states occupy 26 per cent of the land area with Sabah measuring 75,000 km² (28,960 sq miles) in area and Sarawak 125,000 km² (48,266 sq miles). Brunei occupies a mere 5,765 km² (2,226 sq miles).

Naturally Appealing, Culturally Fascinating

Most visitors are captivated as Borneo is a truly enchanting island where it's possible to experience many wonderful natural attractions and a fascinating and diverse culture. Some of the most ecologically rich and biologically complex ecosystems in the world are to be found in Borneo. While logging and the cultivation of plantations have taken their toll on the rainforests, there are still large tracts of unspoiled primary vegetation to explore.

Borneo's flora and fauna are amongst the world's richest. Kinabalu Park, for example, supports some 5,000 known plant species (excluding mosses and liverworts) plus many more that have not even been identified yet. Ornithologists have recorded 664 bird species with 51 being endemic (found only in Borneo). Borneo so impressed the great naturalist Charles Darwin that he called it 'one great luxuriant hothouse made by nature for herself'.

Much of Borneo's reputation for mystery stems from historic accounts of fierce headhunters roaming the forests and tales of swashbuckling adventurers attracted by Borneo's

plentiful resources. While remote villages may still retain their trophy skulls from days gone by, the tribesmen who once were headhunters now live in peace and welcome visitors, as does the population of Borneo generally.

Above: Male Rhinoceros Hornbill, one of eight hornbill species found on Borneo.

Top: The tribal clothes are colourful and richly decorated.

Left: Enjoy evening sunsets in coastal resorts.

Geography

Borneo is in Southeast Asia. It is ringed by various Indonesian islands; Java lies to the south, Sulawesi to the east, Sumatra to the west along with the Malay peninsula and the Philippines to the north. The island straddles the equator and the highest peak is Sabah's Mount Kinabalu (4,101 m/13,455 ft).

Borneo experiences climatic extremes ranging from monsoon conditions especially around the coast to near-freezing temperatures on Mount Kinabalu. The 'wet' monsoon lasts from November to April and the 'dry' period from May to October. The abundant rainforests that cover Borneo naturally thrive on high rainfall, temperature and humidity. The country also boasts cave formations that rival the world's best; those in Sarawak's Mulu National Park are some of the biggest and longest yet discovered.

Below: The slopes of Mount Kinabalu, Borneo's highest peak.

Opposite below: Mulu Caves are some of the world's largest.

Above: Clown Fish and anemones enjoy a symbiotic relationship.

Right: Snorkelling in clear turquoise waters.

It's not only what's found on the land that fascinates visitors but also what can be discovered beneath the tropical waters. Borneo is located between the Indian and Pacific Oceans with the Sulu, Celebes, Java and South China Seas lapping its shores. It is part of the 'Coral Triangle' which extends from the Philippines to the Solomon Islands. These seas support 75 per cent of the world's coral species and more than 3,000 fish species.

Borneo's diverse flora and fauna and its unique geography have inspired the World Wide Fund for Nature (WWF) to set up the Heart of Borneo project to support the three governments in their efforts to establish a network of protected areas. The aim is to prevent further destruction of the Borneo rainforest, and by 2020 it is hoped that one third of Borneo will be set aside as protected areas.

Borneo is sparsely settled. The largest city is Banjarmasin in Southern Kalimantan with some 720,000 residents. The next towns in the top ten are: Samarinda, Kuching, Pontianak, Kota Kinabalu, Balikpapan, Sandakan, Tawau, Miri and Lao Janan.

History

While humans first arrived in Borneo around 45,000 years ago, the ancestors of many of today's indigenous people only settled here about 4,500 years ago. Collectively known as the Dayaks, they colonized coastlines before moving upriver. Europeans arrived in the 16th century and trading began with countries as remote as Portugal, Spain and the Netherlands. Chinese and Indian traders also opened up Borneo to the world.

Sabah was once part of the Sultanate of Brunei and Sulu (Mindanao). In 1882, the British North Borneo Company was formed in order to administer the territory and in 1888 it became the British protectorate of British North Borneo.

By the 19th century Sarawak was a loosely governed territory controlled by the Brunei Sultanate. In 1841, the British adventurer Sir James Brooke helped the sultan to suppress rebellious Sarawakian chiefs and, in return, he was appointed governor. He subsequently became the Rajah of Sarawak and so began the 100-year-long rule of the White Rajahs, essentially a Brooke family dynasty. The last rajah ceded sovereignty to the British in 1946.

The Anglo-Dutch Treaty of 1824 indirectly divided Borneo into British- and Dutch-controlled areas. The Dutch controlled what is present day Kalimantan. The Japanese occupied the whole of Borneo from 1942 to 1945 until they were overcome by Australian forces who landed on the island in the closing months of the Second World War.

After the war, a rising spirit of Malaysian and Indonesian nationalism opposed the re-establishment of the old colonial powers in Borneo. The desire for independence prevailed and Dutch Borneo became part of Indonesia in 1950, while Sarawak and Sabah joined the Malayan Federation in 1963. Brunei gained its independence in 1984.

Right: The memorial chapel to the 'Death March' prisoner-of-war camp in Sandakan.

Left: Communal area of a typical longhouse.

Above: Colourful tribal communities greet guests in some Borneo hotels.

Below: Mosques and water villages are a common sight in Brunei.

The People

Visitors to the Sarawak Cultural Village on the outskirts of Kuching quickly discover that Borneo is an ethnically diverse island of about 15 million people who belong to 32 recognized ethnic groups. Seven main groups have been identified – Barito, Bidayuh, Dusin-Kadazan-Murut, Iban, Kayan-Kenyah, Kelabit-Lun Bawang and Maloh.

The population can be further divided into coastal or inland people with the inland groups (Land Dayaks) being highly tribalized, but low in numbers. Typically they are hunter-gatherers and shifting cultivators (practising a type of agriculture in which the cultivated area is shifted regularly to allow the soil to recover naturally). However, development has changed the traditional lifestyles of most. Many were once animists, although Christianity has been adopted by some communities.

The small tribal population of Penans are one of the last remaining groups of hunter-gatherers in Borneo. Once nomadic in lifestyle, many are now sedentary and live in permanent longhouses.

Coastal communities along the floodplains, rivers and estuaries are more urbanized, typically with higher population densities and employing organized agricultural practices. Fishing and rice farming are common and many people are traders. The majority of the coastal populations are either Malays or Chinese with the main Chinese dialect groups being Hakka, Cantonese, Foochow and Hokkien. English is widely spoken especially in the coastal areas, where some people are bi- or even trilingual.

Right: *A modern day tribal hunter in the forest.*

Above: Animist wood carving.

Right: A heavily-tattooed tribal elder.

Below: Tribal elder showing young visitors how to hunt with a blowpipe.

Left: Young village child surrounded by rattan carrying baskets.

Above: Barbecuing fish in a local market.

Left: Traditional method for pounding rice into flour.

Left: Weaving a traditional cotton textile called 'ikat'.

Below: Native tribeswomen showing a visitor how to make a bead belt.

While many people in Borneo have adopted contemporary lifestyles and dress, others, especially those living upriver in the interior of Borneo, maintain a traditional way of life. They live in longhouses, grow crops and harvest the rainforest for the essentials of life. They make rice wine and weave intricate cotton cloth called *ikat*. It is these communities that hold the greatest fascination for tourists.

The Iban *ikat* reveals a relationship between textiles and a belief in omens and dreams. Motifs used in the textiles have been passed down from generation to generation and they are hand-woven into a cloth known as *pua kumbu*. Natural maroon, brown and black dyes are used to make ceremonial cloth that is keenly sought after by tourists. Natural dyes are also used in tattooing which remains popular in some communities.

Many of the textiles are ceremonial in purpose and are brought out to mark symbolic events in the village or during festivals. One of the most important festivals in Sarawak is *Gawai Dayak* which marks the end of the rice harvest and is celebrated on 1 June. At a similar time, Sabahans celebrate *Pesta Ka'amatan* or the harvest festival to give thanks for a bountiful rice crop.

Unique Habitats

To the casual observer, Borneo may seem like a land that is simply covered in rainforest, but in fact five major forest types can be distinguished – dipterocarp, mangrove and nipa, freshwater swamp, heath, and montane forests.

Dipterocarp Forests

Dipterocarps are named after the plant family Dipterocarpaceae. The name refers to the two-winged seeds that allow efficient dispersal by wind, and this accurately describes most of the 500 species growing here. Dipterocarp forests dominate Borneo and botanists believe that they once covered 80 per cent of the land. They flourish below 900 m (3,000 ft) where soils are not regularly flooded. In its pristine state, such a forest features tall trees and is layered with an understorey, a mid-layer, the canopy and emergents (the tallest trees that stretch above the canopy). Dipterocarp forest is what most tourists picture when they imagine what tropical rainforest or jungle will look like.

Above right: Aerial roots of a tree in a mangrove forest.

Right: Dipterocarp forests feature trees with huge buttresses.

Mangrove and Nipa Coastal Forest

These forests grow in the zone between the land and the sea. As many rivers in Borneo have low gradients, mangrove and nipa coastal forests can extend far inland. Specialized plants adapt to the saline conditions with the most common type being mangroves. Twisted aerial mangrove roots trap nutrients and, when inundated by the tide, they provide suitable conditions for marine life to spawn.

Mangroves are important to commercial fishing as well as helping to protect coasts from erosion and the effects of storm and tsunami damage. Mangroves are replaced by nipa palms as the water becomes less saline. This habitat is virtually impenetrable but villagers do manage to harvest fronds for thatching and matting. Macaques and the Proboscis Monkey live here savouring the high sugar content of the nipa palm buds.

Above: Special glands in mangrove trees concentrate salt and allow it to evaporate.

Right: Several parks in Borneo have raised boardwalks for visitors to gain access to mangrove forests.

Freshwater Swamp Forest

Upriver, freshwater swamp forest replaces mangrove and nipa coastal forest as the water loses its salinity. This type of forest is further divided into riverine and peat forest according to the soils in which they're located. Riverine forest is found near rivers and is nutrient-rich from regular deposits of alluvial silt. High nutrient levels mean that plants grow profusely which results in high wildlife densities.

Riverine forests near Sabah's Lower Kinabatangan River are home to Orang-utans, Bornean Pygmy Elephants, Proboscis Monkeys and many species of birds, amphibians and reptiles. However, plantation crops like oil palm also grow well in these fertile soils and so Borneo's remaining natural forests are under continual threat of clearing to create plantations. Peat swamp forest is less fertile due to the acidity of the soil. It is particularly common in the province of South Kalimantan and in parts of Sarawak. However, it is vulnerable as the timber here can be harvested and the land planted out to oil palm.

Above: Clear water streams are common especially in montane forest.

Left: Heath or 'kerangas' forest is found in some parks like Bako National Park.

Montane Forest

Temperature drops with increasing altitude and above 900 m (3,000 ft), stunted myrtle, laurel and oak species form what is known as montane forest. Tree species are typically shorter than in other types of forests, and mosses and lichens thrive in the misty conditions. Rhododendrons, ferns, orchids and epiphytes are also typical. Sabah's Mount Kinabalu is Borneo's most accessible montane forest.

Left: Mists are common in montane forest.

Marine Environments

There are many beautiful coral reefs and superb diving locations surrounding Borneo. Sipadan Island off Sabah's northeastern coastline is considered by experts to be one of the world's best dive sites. Other good diving islands include Mabul, Lankayan, Mantanani and Layan Layan. Live aboard diving is available as is reef diving just off Miri and wreck diving off Labuan.

Heath Forest

Heath forest has evolved to colonize acidic, sandy soil and plants growing here have adapted to the low levels of available nutrients. Locally, this forest is known as *kerangas* and it is found in various locations from coasts to highlands. One of the most accessible examples is in Sarawak's Bako National Park. Heath forest is dominated by densely packed trees with small leaves that grow into a low, even canopy. Carnivorous pitcher plants are common here.

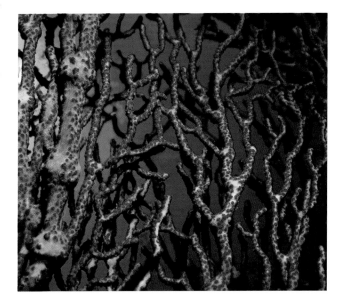

Rght: Colourful corals are found in the seas surrounding Borneo.

Unique Plants

Borneo is considered a world hotspot for botanic diversity. In one study, researchers in Borneo identified more tree species in one 10-ha (25-acre) plot of rainforest than are found in the whole of North America. More than 15,000 plant species, including some 3,000 trees, have been identified. Many of these are found only on the island.

Borneo's rainforests are home to many unusual plants, such as *Alocasia macrorrhiza*, a type of arum which, at 3 m (10 ft) long and 1.9 m (6 ft) wide, has the biggest leaves in the world. Trees like the Menggaris (*Koompassia excelsa*) often grow taller than 60 m (200 ft) and protrude high above the forest canopy.

The island is home to more than 50 species of carnivorous pitcher plants (*Nepenthes* genus) and, in Kinabalu Park alone, ten of them can be found growing on outcrops of rock. Some leaves develop into an extraordinary pitcher-like structure, in which insects become trapped and drown in a sap-like liquid contained in the pitcher. Then nutrients from the decomposing insect bodies are slowly digested by the plant.

Above right: Pitcher plants are commonly found in soils with poor nutrients.

Right: 'Nepenthes rajah', found in Borneo is the largest pitcher plant in the world.

Orchids are also prolific with some 2,500 species being found in Borneo (10 per cent of all known species), with more being discovered by scientists each year. One endemic Kinabalu specimen, Rothschild's Slipper Orchid, is considered the king of the slipper orchids. Sabah Agricultural Park in Tenom is an excellent place to see orchids, plants and a variety of fruit trees.

Above: The entrance to Sabah Agricultural Park at Tenom.

Right: One of many tropical orchids in bloom at the Sabah Agricultural Park.

Rafflesia is a parasitic plant that grows on *Tetrastigma* vines. One species (*R. keithii*) produces the world's largest flower which can be up to 100 cm (40 in) in diameter. These flowers take about nine months to mature into a ball about the size of a small cabbage after which the putrid-smelling bloom opens. However, the flower only lasts for five days or so. Wild blooms are only seen rarely, but the best places to try to catch them are Kinabalu Park and the Rafflesia Centre near Tambunan in Sabah.

Fruits such as durian, *salak* (or snake fruit because its skin resembles that of a snake) and rambutans grow wild in the forests of Borneo, and are harvested either for eating locally or for sale in nearby markets. Durian, the 'king of fruits', is a football-sized, spiky, yellow-green fruit with a thick husk. According to one popular description, it 'tastes like heaven but smells like hell'. Fruit bats, spiderhunter birds and giant honey bees pollinate the flowers of the nine edible species and another 20 non-edible ones.

Many other plants have traditionally been a source of food, medicines, building materials and even clothing for Borneo's native tribes. Scientists are still identifying new species and experts believe that within the rainforest's incredible plant diversity there may be found natural plant compounds that will help to treat current and future medical conditions.

Opposite above left: The spiky durian fruits grow wild and may attain the size of a football.

Opposite above right: The fleshy durian fruit has a soft, creamy texture.

Opposite: Fan palms grow in the luxuriant understory of tropical rainforests.

Right: 'Rafflesia' flowers are the largest in the world.

Opposite: The flower of a common ginger species.

Unique Animals

Borneo is home to many extraordinary and unusual animals. Deforestation and the clearing of land for agriculture are detrimental, especially to the larger animals, and some are now endangered.

While they are also found on Sumatra, Orang-utans are synonymous with Borneo. They are mostly solitary animals that sleep in nests made each night in rainforest trees. Orang-utans are the animals that most tourists come to see and there are several protected areas and rehabilitation centres where this is possible. During forest logging, juveniles may become separated from their mothers and become orphaned. These orphans are taught survival skills in rehabilitation centres before being reintroduced into the wild. Sepilok (Sabah), Matang Wildlife Centre (Sarawak) and Wanariset (East Kalimantan) are notable examples.

It's also possible to see Orang-utans in forests such as the Kinabatangan, Danum Valley and Tabin Wildlife Reserve in Sabah and Sarawak's Batang Ai. In Kalimantan, there are some readily accessible sites, as well as more remote ones. For tourists it is probably best to visit easily accessible national parks such as Kutai, Gunung Palung and Tanjung Puting in Kalimantan's lowlands.

Left: A juvenile Orang-utan swinging across jungle vines.

Above: Visitors at Sepilok getting close to wild Orang-utans.

One of the strangest looking monkeys in Borneo is the Proboscis Monkey. The males have huge noses and barrel-like bellies, and they so resembled the early Dutch colonists that in Kalimantan they were called the Dutch monkey. Regrettably it is now endangered as its habitats dwindle.

Other primates include several leaf monkeys (langurs) such as the Silvered-leaf Monkey, Pig-tailed Macaque, Red-leaf Monkey, Long-tailed Macaque, Gibbon, Slow Loris and Western Tarsier.

Below right: Proboscis Monkeys take prodigious leaps in the forests.

Right: Silvered-leaf Monkey.

Below: Common Macaque.

Borneo Pygmy Elephants are smaller than other Asian elephants. Males grow to 2.5 m (8.2 ft) – other Asian elephants grow to 3 m (9.8 ft) – and they also differ in having longer tails, straighter tusks, shorter trunks and larger ears.

Borneo's rarest large animal is the Sumatran Rhinoceros. Despite being the world's smallest rhino, an adult can weight up to 800 kg (1,765 lb). It has two horns and sparse shaggy hair. Sadly, poaching has taken a deadly toll and the best estimates suggest that maybe only 40 survive in Borneo out of a total wild population of around 275. Tracks of Sumatran Rhinoceros have been recorded in Sabah's Danum Valley and Tabin Wildlife Reserve but sightings are extremely rare.

The Sun Bear is the world's smallest bear – it is only about 1.2 m (4 ft) tall – but it is Borneo's largest carnivore. Mostly nocturnal it is named for a light patch on its chest. Other interesting animals found in Borneo are a variety of bats, shrews, rodents, porcupines, pigs, civet cats and squirrels.

Above: The Large Egret is found along many waterways.

Left: Borneo Pygmy Elephant with young.

Birds are another important wildlife element. Eight species of hornbill live here, namely the Rhinoceros, Wreathed, Helmeted, Wrinkled, Oriental Pied, Asian Black, White-crowned and Bushy-crested Hornbill. They have a unique way of nesting – the female is sealed in a tree hollow and fed through a gap by the male.

Other unique birds to look out for include the Bornean Bristlehead, Bornean Barbet, Whitehead's Trogon and Hose's broadbill. The annual Borneo Bird Festival held in Sandakan in October is a particularly good time for bird watchers to visit Sabah. A new bird species, yet to be named, was recently discovered in Danum Valley. Borneo is on the flight path from the northern to southern hemisphere.

Large animals need not be the sole focus of attention. A wealth of reptiles, flying squirrels, insects, spiders, frogs and butterflies also make Borneo a fascinating place to visit. For instance, the Atlas Moth, the world's largest moth with a wing span of 25 cm (10 in), can be seen here.

Above: Oriental Pied Hornbills.

Below: Atlas Moth.

Land and Resources

Borneo was once largely covered in forests but logging and agriculture have reduced the primary forest cover to around 50 per cent. While the rate of forest clearing has slowed, and ecotourism is becoming more important to the local economy, conservationists have called for the extension and establishment of additional protected areas.

Below: Sago grubs are a delicacy in parts of Borneo.

Some isolated indigenous communities still practise shifting cultivation which involves slashing and burning areas of forest to grow crops, and then moving on to new sites when the soil nutrients become depleted. Others work for logging and mining companies, on plantations or grow upland rice (Sarawak's Bario Highlands rice is considered some of the best). Now vast tracts of Borneo have been cleared for oil palm plantations. While palm oil is a valuable commodity, the plantations are monocultures that are alien to most wildlife.

Above: Fishing communities live in stilt houses over the sea.

Left: Harvesting oil palm bunches.

In Kalimantan, numerous rubber estates and small holdings help to position Indonesia as the world's second largest rubber producer. Mining, especially for coal in areas of Kalimantan, also produces valuable resources but at an environmental cost. Other important cash crops in Borneo include sago, tapioca, cocoa, pepper, tea and coffee.

Coastal wetlands are important for fishing and many local communities are involved in the industry. Sabah's Bajau population were once nomadic, subsistence boat dwellers who fished the Sulu Sea. Many have now given up the nomadic lifestyle, but they are still involved in fishing.

Opposite: Water buffaloes are important for ploughing the cultivated rice fields.

Right: Tea is grown on the lower slopes of Mount Kinabalu.

Adventures and Lifestyle

With such a wild landscape, it's not surprising that Borneo can offer tourists a wealth of thrilling adventures. For some, a forest trek or a river journey proves adventure enough. Others intrepidly choose to explore caves, climb precipitous cliffs, shoot rapids, mountain bike along forest trails and scuba-dive at some of the world's best dive sites.

Climbing Sabah's Mount Kinabalu is one of Borneo's great adventures. The 'via ferrata' (iron road) provides access to the slopes of Mount Kinabalu using a series of rungs, rails and cables on the rock face that allow hikers to experience scenic sections of the mountain that in the past were only available to experienced rock climbers. At 3,800 m (12,470 ft) high, it's billed as the world's highest via ferrata and is guaranteed to get the adrenalin pumping.

In Sarawak, experienced adventurers love to climb the Pinnacles in Mulu National Park. These jagged limestone outcrops are typical of the karst topography found in parts of Borneo. Beneath Mulu's mountainous outcrops there are huge caves that attract both casual cavers and experienced underground explorers.

White-water rafting is becoming more popular and Sabah's Kiulu and Padas Rivers are two of the best destinations for this. The Kiulu is ideal for beginners while the Padas is for those seeking more extreme challenges. In Central Kalimantan, head to Gohong Rawai or Amandit River for similar river-based adventure.

Above: Kayaking around islands off Kota Kinabalu.

Right: Water skiing around the Borneo coastline.

Opposite above: White-water rafting on a raging jungle river.

Opposite below: Climbing the world's highest 'via ferrata' on Mount Kinabalu. Via ferrata is Italian for 'iron road' and describes mountain routes of cables, bridges and ladders that are popular in Europe.

And there is plenty to do for those people who are not necessarily thrill-seekers. More leisurely activities abound, such as bird watching (Sabah especially is recognized as a leading birding destination), sailing, kayaking, parasailing and jungle trekking. The waters surrounding Borneo offer some of world's best scuba and snorkelling sites. Sipadan, Layang-Layang, Mabul and Kapalai provide the best diving.

Golf is popular in urban areas and holiday resorts and many of the world's leading designers have crafted courses through rainforest, skirting near-deserted beaches and stretching up into the foothills. In Sabah, the most challenging courses include Borneo Golf Resort, Sutera Harbour, Nexus Golf Resort, Dalit Bay, Tawau Golf Club, Kinabalu Golf Club and Sandakan Golf Club. Sarawak's 'must play' courses include Damai Golf & Country Club, Eastwood Valley, Hornbill Golf & Jungle Club and Miri Golf Club. In Brunei the Royal Brunei Golf & Country Club and the Empire Golf Club are fit for royalty, but open to all.

Above: Photographing the rainforest from the elevated walkway at Sepilok.

Left: Aerial view of Dalit Bay Golf Course, Sabah.

Other visitors to Borneo are attracted by the indigenous people and wish to participate in cultural events like music and dance festivals and culinary encounters. Two popular music festivals held in Sarawak are Borneo Jazz (May) and the Rainforest World Music Festival (July). Borneo Jazz (formerly the Miri Jazz Festival) hosts a fusion of jazz, blues and roots music that unfolds by the seaside in this oil-rich city. The Rainforest Festival is based in the forest setting of Sarawak Cultural Village near Kuching. Indigenous musicians play alongside leading exponents of world music in a carnival atmosphere with music workshops taking place throughout the day.

Shopping

While typically modern shopping centres are found in the larger cities and towns, Borneo offers discerning shoppers several unique local products. Tribal handicrafts are popular souvenirs since most are still traditionally made, as they have been for centuries, using local materials. Good places to buy them are in markets, which in Borneo are called *tamu*. The best include Sunday's Gaya Street (Kota Kinabalu), Kota Belud Sunday Market, Kuching Weekend Market, Kota Kinabalu's Filipino Market, Miri's Tamu Muhibbah and Banjarmasin's Muara Kuin Floating Market. Shops lining Kuching's Main Bazaar are also worth exploring. Here you can buy something special like carved wooden totems, beads, *ikat* cloth (*pua kumbu*), Tenom coffee, Sabah tea, Sarawak pepper and even clothing made from bark.

Left: The 'sape' is a traditional lute-like instrument found in Sarawak.

Above: Fans enjoying world-class music at the Rainforest World Music Festival, Kuching.

Chapter 2: Sarawak

Sarawak is Malaysia's largest state and home to some 30 indigenous groups with most of the people living in coastal areas. It is renowned for its natural areas and native communities.

Kuching

The Sarawak River divides the Sarawak capital of Kuching. Kuching is one of Borneo's largest cities and was established by the first White Rajah, James Brooke. It is known as 'Cat City' and was named after the green longan fruit which is known locally as *cat's eye* or *mata kuching*. There is a cat monument in the centre of Kuching and a Cat Museum at Petra Jaya just north of the city.

A cruise boat operating as the Sarawak River Cruise makes several daily trips along the river. The Courthouse and Brooke Memorial are also located along the Waterfront. Kuching Courthouse is a delightful colonial building dating back to 1874 and is architecturally noteworthy for its grand columns, shaded verandahs, courtyards and clock tower.

Sarawak Museum, dating back to 1891 is considered one of Asia's finest. There are two sections connected via a footbridge and both house tribal artefacts with sections on beads, basketry, textiles, metalwork and ceramics among other displays.

Above: Cats are celebrated throughout Kuching, Sarawak.

Left: The Kuching Waterfront is lined with wooden sampans called 'tambang' that ferry people across the river.

Above: Fort Marguerita sits on the northern riverbank. It was built in 1879 by Charles Brooke, Sarawak's second White Rajah. It is named after his wife Rani Margaret and it once guarded the settlement against pirate attack. Not far downstream is the Astana which was once the original home of the White Rajahs and is now the State Governor's official residence. It is not open to the public. These stately buildings are surrounded by local villages that have changed little over time. The new Sarawak State Legislative Assembly Hall is a crown-like structure that now dominates the riverscape.

Right: The striking red Tua Pek Kong Temple near the Hilton Hotel is in stark contrast to an adjoining modern shopping mall.

Left: The city's commercial heart is located on the southern riverbank as are several international hotels including the Pullman and Hilton.

Above and left: The riverbank has been rejuvenated as the Waterfront and is recognized as one of Asia's finest public spaces and urban regeneration projects. It features tree-lined gardens, an esplanade, solar-powered lights, historic plaques, performance spaces, sculptures and musical fountains. Several old buildings including the Sarawak Shipping Company have been renovated and an elevated platform provides panoramic river views.

Left: Chillies at Kuching market. Discover many local treats at the weekend markets located along Jalan Satok just out of the city centre.

Right: India Street Pedestrian Mall derives its name from the fact that the street has historically been occupied by Indian shops. Another popular place to explore on foot is Jalan Carpenter with its narrow shop lots, restaurants and coffee shops.

Left and right: There are plenty of places to eat. Renovated old godowns which were once warehouses for storing goods offloaded from river barges now line the Waterfront. Today, this Main Bazaar is full of restaurants, bars, handicraft stores, tour agencies and shops selling local delicacies such as bird's nests. Two popular local dishes are 'laksa' (left) a popular spicy noodle soup and barbecued fish (right).

Around Kuching

There are various natural and cultural attractions close to Kuching. These range from national parks to longhouses, a cultural village, pleasant beaches, golf courses and dolphin watching on Santubong River. Bako and Kubah National Parks are within an hour by car of Kuching as are the Orang-utan centres of Matang and Semenggoh.

Above and left: Sarawak's Cultural Village at Damai is home to seven of the communities which call Borneo home and it is culturally sensitive, visually exciting and educationally fascinating.
In July, the Rainforest World Music Festival offers another cultural facet of Sarawak life.

Right: Many visitors head to the beaches and resorts of Damai for some rest and recreation. Mount Santubong (810 m/2,657 ft) towers overhead and lures intrepid mountain climbers. Others head off along the Santubong River to get a glimpse of the highly endangered and elusive Irrawaddy Dolphin. Sighting of fins is as much as will be seen as they don't breach the surface. Visitors can also see coastal mangroves and fishing villages.

Sibu and the Rejang River

For a journey into the 'heart of Borneo' an upriver trip on the Rejang River from the logging boom town of Sibu to Pelagus Rapids is one of the world's last frontier river adventures. Journeys on Malaysia's longest river start in the bustling city of Sibu which is serviced by direct flights from Kuala Lumpur and Kuching. Sibu's riverside markets, a seven-storey Chinese pagoda and tropical fruit farm on the outskirts of town are the tourist highlights.

Travel on local ferries or take the luxurious five-day return trip on the 'N.V. Orient Pandaw' for a glimpse of the river which is the lifeline for upriver communities.

Above: A Melanau native traditional longhouse at Lamin Dana.

Right: Visit communities such as Kanowit, Song, Kapit and Belaga before travelling on wooden canoes to explore remote tributaries. Here, Iban tribe members are pictured at their longhouse in Batang Ai with an elder holding a fighting cock.

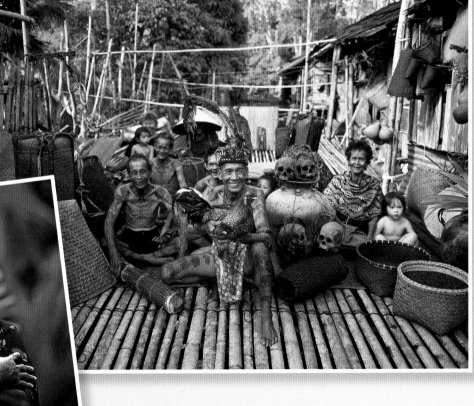

Left: An Orang Ulu woman displays traditional tattoos on her hands and arms and extended ear lobes.

The North – Miri

Malaysia's first oil well was spudded by Shell here in 1910 and so began what is today Malaysia's most valuable industry. The original wooden oil rig sits high above the modern city on Canada Hill and a small but interactive petroleum museum provides detailed information on the oil industry and early life in Miri.

Today, the drilling is done offshore but Miri is still very much an oil town and service centre. Its proximity to Brunei means that it's also a popular party town for those who live in the neighbouring alcohol-free sultanate. Miri's nightlife is lively, colourful and active. There are several well-established bars with some offering live band entertainment.

This page: Canada Hill overlooking Miri is home to Malaysia's first oil well. Known as the Grand Old Lady (top) it stands high beside the Petroleum Museum (centre) which is an interactive learning experience about the oil industry. The city and beaches stretch along the South China Sea below Canada Hill (left).

Top and above right: While many visitors transit here on the way to Mulu Caves and the Sarawak interior, some pleasant beachside resorts make this a good place to rest at the end of a north Sarawak adventure. Brighton Beach (Taman Selera) is home to Miri Marina, seafood restaurants, picnic areas and two international-standard hotels – Miri Marriott Resort and Spa and ParkCity Everly Hotel. The latter is the venue for the Borneo Jazz Festival in May.

Left: Miri Marina and lighthouse.

Top and above right: Miri also has several attractive parks with the grand Miri City Fan and Japanese Garden being popular places for quiet relaxation. The ornately decorated Lian Hua San Temple in suburban Krokop is the largest Taoist place of worship in Southeast Asia.

Left: Surprisingly, even to seasoned divers, Miri has several well-recognized dive sites just offshore. Visibility is mostly good around shallow coral gardens and there's even a wreck to explore.

Left: Excellent seafood, tribal markets and handicrafts, diving, some 30 ethnic communities and golf also add to Miri's appeal.

Right: Being a service centre, there are several shopping centres and a local handicrafts outlet selling items like woven beads. One of the most colourful markets is Tamu Muhibbah where upriver products are sold. The fish market in the city near Tua Pek Hong Temple is just as interesting.

The Interior

In the past, the only way into Sarawak's interior was via arduous river journeys. For better or worse, logging trails have opened up parts of the interior. Many isolated communities also have simple airstrips where Twin Otters operated by MASWings bring in vital supplies as well as flying people out into the wider world. Long Banga, Long Seridan, Long Akah and Long Lellang ('long' meaning the confluence of two rivers) are as isolated as any but can be visited by intrepid travellers prepared for some discomfort.

Above and right: *Ba'kelalan is another remote community that grows famous upland rice as well as possibly the only crop of apples in the whole region. Many of the communities in the interior are Christian, and conservative and traditional values reign supreme. Staying with the locals and going on forest walks are highlights.*

Above: Communities like Bario and Ba'kelalan have reasonable tourism infrastructure with the former being popular with backpackers. Bario in the Kelabit Highlands is ringed by forested hills and various tracks make it suitable for extended jungle treks. It's possible to fly into Bario, trek overland for several days staying in longhouses and then fly out of places like Long Lellang.

Natural Places

Forestry Department Sarawak administers 15 national parks, five wildlife sanctuaries and five reserves (places too small to be national parks). Some one million hectares (2,471,000 acres) of forest or 8 per cent of Sarawak is protected as national parks. These include archaeological sites, natural features, endangered animal habitats and wildlife rehabilitation centres. The National Parks Booking Office in Kuching is the best information and booking centre for all these parks.

Bako National Park

Bako is Sarawak's oldest national park having been gazetted in 1957 to protect its stunning coastal scenery (bottom right), varied forest communities and associated wildlife. Bako is a 'must see' because it offers so much variety and is close to Kuching. While only covering 2,727 ha (6,738 acres), its landscape varies from beaches to mangroves, dipterocarp forest, rocky headlands, peat swamp forest and heath forest. Proboscis Monkeys and Long-tailed Macaques (top right) are commonly sighted in the mangroves and a network of trails radiating from the accommodation chalets enables visitors to traverse many areas. Pitcher plants grow prolifically within heath forest.

Similajau National Park

Bintulu is home to Malaysia's booming liquid natural gas industry and the wettest place in Malaysia with an annual rainfall of about 540 cm (213 in). Similajau, just 20 km (12 1/2 miles) to the north protects 7,067 ha (17,463 acres) of coastal, heath, mixed dipterocarp and peat forests. Marked trails provide access and apart from crocodiles, there are gibbons, langurs and macaques living here and some 185 bird species including seven species of hornbill. Most visitors make day-visits to the park from Bintulu.

Kubah National Park

Kubah, 30 km (18.6 miles) west of Kuching, adjoins Matang Wildlife Centre with its display of Orang-utans and other orphaned wildlife. Matang has taken over much of the function of the Semenggoh Wildlife Rehabilitation Centre but both are still good for viewing orphaned Orang-utans being rehabilitated to be returned to the wild. Several forest trails through Kubah enable visitors to explore the 2,230-ha (5,510-acre) park including the 800-m- (2,625-ft-) high summit of Mount Sempati. There are 90 palm species in the park with 16 being endemic to Borneo. Accommodation is available.

Batang Ai National Park

Batang Ai is located 250 km (155 miles) from Kuching in the southwest of Sarawak near the Kalimantan border. Some 24,000 ha (59,300 acres) of dipterocarp forest surround a lake formed when the river was dammed for a hydro-electric project. It's best to visit the park on an organized trip and stay in the Hilton Resort (below) or head upriver to the eco-friendly Nanga Sumpa Lodge and Iban Longhouse. The forests are home to Orang-utans, gibbons, hornbills, deer, wild pigs and Clouded Leopards.

Gunung Gading National Park

Gunung (Mount) Gading, two-hour's drive from Kuching, is located near the coast at Lundu. Lowland dipterocarp forest covers the mountainous 4,106 ha (10,146 acre) park and rafflesia flowers (above) are the star attraction. Ranger assistance is required in locating these as only a few flower each year and then just for a few days. Waterfalls and extended trails will appeal to adventurous explorers and the traditional Bidayuh roundhouse that acts as a visitor centre is architecturally interesting. Visitors can stay in park accommodation and cool off on nearby deserted beaches at Siar and Pandan Lundu.

Above: An Iban tribesman using a blowpipe.

Left: The verandah of a longhouse.

Below: The waters of Batang Ai.

Niah Caves National Park

In 1958, archaeologists discovered human remains in the limestone caves here (above) that date back 40,000 years. While access to the archaeological remains of cave paintings and wooden coffins (left) is restricted, there is a lot to see and the cave formations are fascinating. They are also home to millions of swiftlets and bats so there are mounds of accumulated guano. The caves in the 3,140-ha (7,759-acre) park are accessible via an elevated boardwalk and park accommodation is available. Niah Caves are located between Miri and Bintulu with the closest airport being Miri, 115 km (70 miles) to the north.

Lambir Hills National Park

This 6,952-ha (17,178-acre) park, 24 km (15 miles) south of Miri is best known for its flora, especially stands of mixed dipterocarp forest. Heath forest and pitcher plants are also supported here on the nutrient-deficient sandstone soil. These forests are home to Long-tailed Macaques and deer as well as some 150 bird species. A 40-m- (130-ft-) high forest tower along the Pantu Trail is ideal for observing some of these birds and there are several small waterfalls and bathing pools (opposite). Accommodation is available in and around the park.

Gunung Mulu National Park

While Gunung (Mount) Mulu Park is named after its highest peak at 2,376 m (7,795 ft), it's the subterranean features of this UNESCO World Heritage Site that lure most visitors. Deer Cave is the world's largest cave passage and the Sarawak Chamber is the largest chamber in the world at 700 m (2,300 ft) in length, 300 m (985 ft) in width and 70 m (230 ft) in height. Many caves haven't even been explored so speleologists eagerly anticipate more discoveries.

Most visitors fly in from Miri to explore four caves – Deer (below left), Lang, Wind and Clearwater which are accessible via raised boardwalks and river journeys (above right). The nightly exodus of millions of bats from Deer Cave is one of Borneo's great natural wonders. In addition to seeking out the park's flora and fauna, many adventures – such as mountain biking, rock climbing, jungle trekking, rafting, kayaking and visiting longhouses – are possible.

Accommodation in and around the park ranges from dormitories at park headquarters to homestays and the relative luxury of the Mulu Marriott Resort & Spa (opposite above).

Right: Mulu's rainforests are home to many lizard species.

Above: The Pinnacles, Mulu National Park.

Above: Egrets roost alongside rivers.

Chapter 3: Sabah

Sabah is Malaysia's second largest state with Kota Kinabalu (simply called 'KK') being the modern capital. The state is known as 'The Land Below the Wind' as it is located south of the typhoon belt. Once known as Jesselton, the capital was mostly razed to the ground by Allied bombs at the end of the Second World War. It was rebuilt and in 1967 it was renamed Kota Kinabalu. What it lacks in terms of historic buildings it makes up for in being a lively city with a vibrant ethnic mix and several resorts near the city centre.

Kota Kinabalu

The city faces the South China Sea and its reclaimed waterfront is lined with hotels, apartments, marinas, restaurants, shops, bars and cafés. Not surprisingly, fresh seafood features on most restaurant menus. The best views of the waterfront, city and offshore islands are from Signal Hill just behind the Sabah Tourism Office.

Sabah Museum is a modern building on a knoll not far from the State Mosque. Architects refer to it as an example of vernacular revivalism as the design is based upon a traditional Rungus longhouse which has outward-sloping walls beneath a broad sloping roof. It houses displays on the state's ethnography, archaeology, natural history and handicrafts. Several examples of traditional local houses are located in the museum's Heritage Village.

The glistening golden dome of the Sabah State Mosque dominates the skyline. Kinabalu City Mosque built in suburban Likas in 2000 seems to float on a lake and is often referred to as the 'floating mosque'.

Left: The mangroves of the Kota Kinabalu Wetland Centre in Likas cover 24 ha (59 acres) and are home to 80 species of resident and migratory birds such as sandpipers, egrets, herons and kingfishers.

Below and opposite: The integrated Sutera Harbour development near the city centre includes two hotels, a marina, 36-hole golf courses, housing estates, a sports complex, restaurants and bars. It has helped put the city on regional tourism maps.

Above: Relaxing at Gayana Eco Resort off Kota Kinabalu.

Above and top: Kota Kinabalu's sunsets over the South China Sea and islands are legendary. Soak them up at a bar or restaurant along The Waterfront and Esplanade. Activities become livelier later in the evening as the bars and clubs move into top gear.

Above right: Gaya Street's Sunday market is one large urban 'tamu' that spreads along the street and into several side streets. There's not much that's not sold here and it's liveliest early in the morning until noon. Nearby, the range of handicrafts in the Filipino Market is extraordinary. Being so close to Mindanao in the Philippines, these markets are named after the Filipino immigrants who operate many stalls here.

Around Kota Kinabalu

Tunku Abdul Rahman Park, comprising five islands, is located just off the Kota Kinabalu coastline. Accommodation is available on Manukan, Gaya and Mamutik Islands while Sapi is popular for day visitors seeking sun, sand and snorkelling.

Train enthusiasts will enjoy riding the train to Tenom and back with the possibility of an overnight stay in Tenom in order to visit the Sabah Agricultural Park and Tenom Orchid Centre. Alternatively, take a tourist steam train between Tanjung Aru and Papar on the North Borneo Railway.

Monsopiad Cultural Village, beside the Penampang River, 16 km (10 miles) from the city centre, is the former home of a fearsome local Kadazan warrior. In addition to learning about the culture, the house of skulls with 42 'trophies' is what attracts most visitors.

Above: There are several resorts between Kota Kinabalu and Tauran to the north with both the Nexus Karambunai and Shangri-La Rasa Ria Resorts having beachfront locations and adjoining golf courses.

Above: The North Borneo Railway is a nostalgic steam train journey that operates several times per week from near Kota Kinabalu to Papar, a return distance of 120 km (75 miles). This private steam train only operates on part of the public railway line that extends all the way to Tenom.

Eastern Sabah

Lahad Datu and Tawau are gateways to East Sabah. Lahad Datu attracts nature lovers wishing to explore the Maliau Basin, Danum Valley and Tabin while diving is the main reason many fly into Tawau.

Sipadan is Malaysia's only deepwater oceanic island sitting 600 m (1,970 ft) above the ocean floor and home to turtles, sharks, rays, wrasses and corals. Divers fly into Tawau and then drive one hour to Semporna to access the major dive sites of Sipadan, Mabul and Kapalai.

Right: Lion Fish are commonly sighted.

Above: Sipadan Island off Sabah's east coast is Malaysia's only oceanic island rising some 600 m (1,970 ft) from the seabed in the Celebes Sea.

Above: Danum Valley and the Maliau Basin are two of Sabah's remotest protected areas but accessible via Lahad Datu. Both have a 'lost world' setting with Maliau Basin being only 'discovered' in 1947 and being first explored in 1988. It is as isolated as it gets but five-day treks are available into this pristine rainforest and to the majestic Maliau Falls. Danum Valley is slightly more accessible but only just. High-end ecotourism facilities at the Borneo Rainforest Lodge are available for overnight visitors to explore pristine rainforest, streams and waterfalls. A canopy walk and night safari add to the adventure.

Above, centre and below: Just north of Lahad Datu, Tabin Wildlife Reserve is home to rhinos, elephants and wild cattle as well an extensive birdlife and many small mammals. Several low mud volcanoes are important 'salt licks' that attract various animals. Get close to nature by staying in Tabin Wildlife Resort (above) and going on nature treks (left).

Northern Sabah

Visitors fly into the region via Sandakan Airport and from here they fan out seeking out experiences in nature at Sepilok Orang-utan Rehabilitation Centre and the Rainforest Interpretation Centre. Sandakan is also the departure point for the Kinabatangan River and Gomantong Caves.

Sandakan was once the state capital and home to the infamous 'Death March' prison during the Second World War. Sandakan Memorial Park on the outskirts of town is a chilling reminder of the atrocities. The city centre was virtually destroyed by Allied bombings at the end of the war.

Above: Kudat is the port for accessing Pulau Banggi, Malaysia's largest island. It and four surrounding islands support mangroves, coral gardens and sea grasses which are important habitats for turtles, dugongs and monitor lizards.

Above: The small village of Sukau is the gateway to the Kinabatangan and its tributary, the Menanggul, which is considered one of the best places in Borneo to see wildlife. Ecotourists travel up the narrow tributary in small boats to see Proboscis Monkeys, macaques, Orang-utans, reptiles, elephants, crocodiles and birds. Eco lodges are sparsely scattered along the Kinabatangan.

Above: Guide pointing out elephant tracks in the Kinabatangan.

Above: *Juvenile Proboscis Monkeys.*

Right: *For a totally wild experience, adventurers head to the Lower Kinabatangan River, stopping at Gomantong Caves on the way. Gomantong is home to millions of swiftlets and bats which roost here. Swiftlet nests are a prized delicacy in Chinese dishes such as bird's nest soup and skilled climbers harvest the nests. The large caves are as impressive as the mounds of guano are oppressive.*

Right: *Proboscis Lodge on the banks of the Kinabatangan River.*

Right and below: Many visitors fly in from Kota Kinabalu for the day to see Sepilok's Orang-utans but there is much more to do in the area. Visitors can get close to orphaned Orang-utans which are being retrained to be reintroduced to the wild.

Next door in the Rainforest Discovery Centre an elaborate elevated walkway through the rainforest is perfect for seeing birdlife and small animals scurrying around the canopy.

Above: Visitors can see the home where American author Agnes Keith wrote 'Land Below the Wind' and then enjoy croquet and cream teas at the nearby English Tea House. Agnes Keith arrived from California in what was then British North Borneo in 1934, as the wife of Harry Keith, the Conservator of Forests. She fell in love with Sabah and the Sabahan people, and her book paints a vivid picture of her experiences as the only American living in a pre-war colonial outpost. Agnes and Harry lived here until they were interned by the Japanese occupiers in 1942.

Left: Deserted beaches around Kudat near the northernmost tip of Borneo.

Islands

Several islands surround Borneo but few have large settlements. Most provide a Robinson Crusoe image of sun-drenched beaches and turquoise waters. Many are wildlife sanctuaries while others cater to divers.

Below: Aerial view of Pulau Sapi off Kota Kinabalu.

Left: The 90-km² (35-sq mile) island of Labuan to the west of the Sabah coastline is a federal territory administered from Kuala Lumpur. It is also a tax-free haven, trade-free zone and an international offshore financial centre. Many mainlanders come here for its duty-free goods while tourists choose to visit the Commonwealth War Cemetery or to go wreck diving in the surrounding waters.

Opposite: Lankayan Island northwest of Sandakan offers beautiful reef swimming and snorkelling in shimmering, shallow turquoise waters.

This page: Turtle Island National Park, in the Sulu Sea, 40 km (25 miles) north of Sandakan is, as its name suggests, important for turtles. On most nights Green (below left) and Hawksbill Turtles come onto the beaches of the three-island park to lay their eggs and afterwards leave tracks in the sand as they return to the sea (left). Accommodation, a hatchery (below) and interpretation facilities on Seligaan Island enable a handful of ecotourists to enjoy this special phenomenon.

This page: Lankayan Island is a mere speck in the Sulu Sea with just one resort, the Lankayan Island Resort. With accommodation for just 50 guests, it is popular with divers and those who want to escape the madding crowd.

The Interior and Kinabalu Park

Many parts of the Sabah interior are impenetrable forest. However, there are several accessible tourist attractions. Tambunan Rafflesia Reserve in the Crocker Range has an excellent interpretive display on the world's largest flower. Rangers lead walks to flowers that are in bloom.

Sabah's most famous park, Kinabalu Park, covers an area of 750 km² (290 sq miles) and includes Malaysia's highest peak of Mount Kinabalu at 4,101 m (13,455 ft). One of its great attributes is that several parts of the park are accessible to visitors. The peak is sacred land to the local Dusun people and was first climbed by Sir Hugh Low in 1851. Plants collected on this ascent drew scientific attention to the vast numbers of different species here. This incredible diversity led to the establishment of the national park in 1964 and then to its recognition in 2000 as a UNESCO World Heritage Site.

These pages: Mount Kinabalu is a plutonic dome of igneous origin that was thrust up through the Earth's crust some 10 million years ago. During the ice ages of 100,000 years ago the mostly granite rock was scoured by glaciation and the smooth slopes near the summit are evidence of this. Snow falls are rare, although ice is not uncommon.

Climatic conditions vary greatly from the base to the summit with conditions at the summit being so harsh that only the hardiest plants are able to survive. Rhododendrons and conifers dominate near the top but not on the summit itself which is the domain of tough grasses, mosses and lichens. Plant life is limited here not only by the severe climate, but also by the lack of soil on the exposed rocks.

Above: Good facilities make Kinabalu one of Borneo's most visited parks. There is a range of accommodation options (including Laban Rata on the mountain climb) in and around the park as well as a shop, restaurants and guide services. There are two recognized mountain ascents – the main Summit Trail via Laban Rata and the newer Mesilau Trail. Numbers are limited each day and bookings well in advance are essential, as are the services of a mountain guide.

Close by are Poring Hot Springs where naturally heated spring water provides soothing relief after an ascent of Mount Kinabalu. Ranau and Kundasang, located just outside Kinabalu Park, provide accommodation for park visitors.

Above and left: Being a world hot spot for diversity, there are many impressive biological features in the park – 100 species of mammals, over 300 bird species and 5,000 plant species including rare orchids.

Opposite: Many visitors come to the park to admire its flora and fauna, to make the two-day climb to the summit or to enjoy adventurous activities like ascending the 'via ferrata' up the side of the mountain. Each October, the Kinabalu International Climbathon attracts speed merchants who race from base to summit and back, with the record currently being two hours, 33 minutes. Pictured is a competitor climbing Mount Kinabalu in the annual climbathon.

Chapter 4: Brunei Darussalam

The tiny oil-rich independent sultanate of Brunei Darussalam occupies just 5,765 km² (2,226 sq miles) (less than 1 per cent of Borneo's landmass). However, due to the discovery of oil in 1906, its per capita income is one of the highest in the world. Previous Brunei sultans controlled the whole of Borneo along with parts of the Philippines and now the current Sultan administers the most economically valuable part.

Once a British colony, it is now an Islamic state whose 400,000 citizens are ruled by the Sultan. Geographically, Brunei consists of two unconnected parts both of which are surrounded by the Malaysian state of Sarawak.

Above and top: Bandar Seri Begawan, the capital and largest settlement, features a water village called Kampung Ayer which is accessible by water taxi. Houses here are perched on wooden piers and are connected by a maze of walkways and bridges.

This page: On the edge of the water village is Omar Ali Saifuddien Mosque (above), one of the region's landmark structures. Built in 1958, it is an elegant sight and is constructed from the finest imported materials. It sits beside a lagoon and is best viewed at twilight. A replica 16th-century mahligai barge is used for religious ceremonies.

In the heart of the capital, the Royal Regalia Building houses state treasures, ceremonial paraphernalia and historical documents. Brunei History Centre is nearby and is another source of historic documents and genealogy of Brunei royalty. Lapau and Dewan Majlis is where the present Sultan was crowned in 1968. The city's most impressive sight, however, is the Istana Nurul Imam or royal palace. With 1,788 rooms, it is the world's largest residential palace. It looks best at sunset when its golden domes are reflected in the waters of the Brunei River.

The Brunei Museum houses an important collection of Chinese ceramics unearthed from the former site of Brunei Town. Bronze cannons, a natural history collection, Islamic art and an oil and gas display complete the collection.

This page: Despite Brunei society being strictly conservative, there are several beaches including Serasa where watersports such as kayaking, para-sailing (below), windsurfing and sailing are popular with some good diving offshore (top).

Much of Brunei is untouched jungle that supports some of Asia's best primary rainforest. The jewel in this natural ecosystem is Ulu Temburong National Park which is only accessible by boat. In approaching the park via a water taxi, bus and longboat, visitors will pass through riverine habitats where Proboscis Monkeys may be sighted. Adventurous travellers can enjoy floating down jungle streams (above).

This page: There is huge ecotourism potential here with activities like river rafting and tubing as well as jungle trekking being offered. Park accommodation enables visitors to commune closely with nature.

There is an extensive network of boardwalks leading from park headquarters through the lowland dipterocarp forest. One of the highlights is to discover the rainforest canopy via a large tower and walkway situated some 50 m (164 ft) above the rainforest floor. In addition to the plants, there is a wonderful diversity of birdlife and booming gibbons can be heard in the distance.

Chapter 5: Indonesian Kalimantan

Kalimantan occupies about 65 per cent of Borneo but travelling here is a more difficult proposition than the rest of Borneo because the infrastructure isn't as well developed. For adventurous travellers this means fewer tourists, and much of the Indonesian territory is considered frontier travel requiring longer time and offering less comfort than the rest of Borneo.

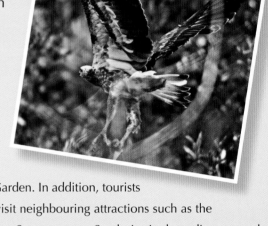

This vast region is divided into West, Central and East Kalimantan with the only road of substance connecting Banjarmasin in southeastern Kalimantan to Sangkulirang in East Kalimantan. Apart from this, it's mostly river travel, coastal journeys or small plane access to remote airstrips.

Balikpapan is the second largest city in the province of East Kalimantan. It is an important centre for the petroleum, mining and timber industries. There are many attractions in Balikpapan such as the beaches at Melawai and Manggar Segarasari, Bekapai Park, Wanawisata Garden and the Agro Tourism Garden. In addition, tourists can also visit neighbouring attractions such as the Orang-utan Sanctuary at Semboja Lodge, dive around Derawan Islands and canoe along the Kandilo River to see various primate species.

Tarakan in northern East Kalimantan and Pontianak in West Kalimantan are popular points of entry because of their proximity to the East Malaysian states of Sabah and Sarawak.

Banjarmasin is the capital of South Kalimantan and known as 'River City' as it lies at the confluence of the Barito and Martapura Rivers. It is an important port for exporting oil, coal, timber, gold and diamonds. Many houses are located over the water and the floating markets are very colourful.

Above: *Immature White-breasted Sea Eagle.*

Left: *Ecotourism is important in Kalimantan.*

Opposite: *Orang-utans are found in Central Kalimantan and several smaller areas in East Kalimantan.*

Above: The national parks of Kalimantan aren't as accessible as those along the western part of Borneo. Those of interest in Kalimantan include Tanjung Puting (415,000 ha/1,025,487 acres) and Gunung Palung National Park (90,000 ha/222,400 acres). Tanjung Puting is in southern Central Kalimantan on a low-lying peninsula and is home to Proboscis Monkeys. While it supports various stands of dipterocarp, heath, peat swamp and mangrove forest, much of the primary forest is degraded. Core areas are protected and it remains an important Orang-utan habitat. Camp Leakey is an important rehabilitation centre. The park is also a UNESCO Biosphere Reserve and home to Clouded Leopards, Sun Bears, crocodiles, hornbills, deer and macaques. There are also some 100,000 people living on the park fringes and illegal activities threaten the park's biological integrity.

Above: Lotus flower found in wetlands.

Below: Insects such as damsel flies are important to the forest ecosystem.

Sebangau Wildlife Sanctuary is located in a threatened peat swamp forest in Central Kalimantan which is home to Orang-utans that may number 4,000 in total. WWF is working with the local Dayak community to improve the infrastructure and access for ecotourists while trying to minimize the effects of logging.

Gunung Palung has problems with illegal logging, poaching and the effects of forest fires. It is recognized for its diversity of plant communities ranging from coastal mangroves to freshwater swamps and montane forests. The park is home to about 10 per cent of the world's Orang-utans and is well known for its primate research. Access is difficult as the park is three hours from Ketapang, near Sukadana.

Right: Buttressed roots are a common feature of large forest trees.

Getting About

For a remote and isolated island, public transport to access Borneo's main tourist attractions, especially in Sabah and Sarawak, is reasonably well developed. The main international gateway airports are Kota Kinabalu (Sabah), Kuching (Sarawak), Bandar Seri Begawan (Brunei) and Balikpapan (Kalimantan).

There are international flights from Malaysia, Indonesia, Singapore, Hong Kong, Australia, Korea and Taiwan to various parts of Borneo. Airlines such as AirAsia, Malaysia Airlines, Royal Brunei Airlines and Garuda International have flights into Borneo with the main regional gateways being Kuala Lumpur, Singapore and Jakarta.

Some remote villages have airports as a community service and lifeline for the villagers to access the world. Fleets of small aircraft service these communities with MASWings flying to remote settlements in Sabah and Sarawak such as Ba'kelalan, Bario, Lawas, Lahad Datu and

Long Seridan. The alternative for villagers is either a long river or dirt road journey.

In other parts of Borneo, the main transportation is via boat along the large rivers of Kalimantan like Kapuas (1,143 km/710 miles), Barito (900 km/560 miles) and Mahakam (775 km/482 miles). In Sabah, the Kinabatangan (560 km/348 miles) and in Sarawak, the Rejang (563 km/350 miles) and Baram (371 km/230 miles) are the longest rivers and main arteries for people moving from the coast to the interior. Long, sleek and noisy aluminium boats ply the deeper rivers but in the smaller and shallower ones, it may be a wooden, paddle-powered sampan that gets adventurous travellers to their destination.

Buses, bikes and 4 x 4 vehicles fill in the gaps and connect communities. Most of the roads grip the coastal areas although the road from Kota Kinabalu to Sandakan in Sabah traverses the highlands. There is an efficient public bus network to and from larger communities.

Borneo's only train operates from Tanjung Aru to Tenom via Beaufort. It is one of the great regional train journeys and passes along the picturesque Padas River. A tourist steam train also operates on part of this route.

Resources

Contacts

The following websites will prove useful in discovering more about Borneo.

Asian Overland Services: www.asianoverland.com.my

Borneo Bird Festival: www.borneobirdfestival.com

Borneo Rhino Alliance: www.borneorhinoalliance.org

Brunei Tourism: www.bruneitourism.com

Forestry Department Sarawak:
    www.forestry.sarawak.gov.my

Indonesia Tourism: www.indonesia-tourism.com

Mountain Torq (via ferrata Mount Kinabalu):
    www.mountaintorq.com

Pandaw River Cruises: www.pandaw.com

Sabah Parks: www.sabahparks.org.my

Sabah Tourism: www.sabahtourism.com

Sarawak National Parks: www.forestry.sarawak.gov.my

Sarawak Tourism: www.sarawaktourism.com

World Wide Fund for Nature Malaysia (WWFM):
    www.wwfm.org.my

Airlines

AirAsia: www.airasia.com

Garuda International: www.garuda-indonesia.com

Malaysia Airlines: www.malaysiaairlines.com

MASWings: www.maswings.com.my

Royal Brunei Airlines: www.bruneiair.com

References

Davidson, G.W.H. and C.A. Yeap. 2010. *Naturalist's Guide to the Birds of Malaysia and Singapore*. John Beaufoy Publishing.

Garbutt, N. and C. Prudente. 2006. *Wild Borneo*. New Holland.

Keith, A. 1939. *Land Below the Wind*. Little, Brown Book Group.

Moore, W. and G. Cubitt. 2003. *This is Malaysia*. New Holland.

Payne, J. and C. Prudente. 2010. *Wild Sabah: The Magnificent Wildlife & Rainforests of Malaysian Borneo*. John Beaufoy Publishing.

Phillipps Q. and K. Phillipps. 2009. *Phillipp's Field Guide to the Birds of Borneo: Sabah, Sarawak, Brunei and Kalimantan*. John Beaufoy Publishing.

Phillips, A. and F. Liew. 2000. *Globetrotter Visitor's Guide, Kinabalu Park, Sabah, Malaysian Borneo*. New Holland.

Raby, P. 2002. *Alfred Russel Wallace – A Life*. Pimlico.

Silver, L. M. 1995. *A Conspiracy of Silence*. Sally Milner Publishing.

Acknowledgements

The author would like to thank Sabah Tourism and Sarawak Tourism for their kind assistance.

The publishers and the author would like to express special thanks to Ken Scriven for his advice and support during the preparation of this book.

About the Author

David Bowden is a freelance photojournalist based in Malaysia specializing in travel and the environment. While Australian, he's been in Asia for longer than he can remember and returns to his home country as a tourist. When he's not travelling the world, he enjoys relaxing with his equally adventurous wife Maria and daughter Zoe.

Index

JOHN BEAUFOY PUBLISHING

First published in the United Kingdom in 2011 by John Beaufoy Publishing,
11 Blenheim Court, 316 Woodstock Road, Oxford OX2 7NS, England
www.johnbeaufoy.com

10 9 8 7 6 5 4 3 2

Great care has been taken to maintain the accuracy of the information contained in this work.
However, neither the publishers nor the author can be held responsible for any consequences
arising from the use of the information contained therein.

ISBN 978-1-906780-50-0

Edited, designed and typeset by Stonecastle Graphics
Cartography by William Smuts
Project management by Rosemary Wilkinson

Printed and bound in Malaysia by Times Offset (M) Sdn Bhd.

All photos by David Bowden except for:
C.V. Chong, Sabah Tourism (p67). David Kirkland, Sabah Tourism (p3 bottom left, p5 top right, p27 top, p51 centre &
bottom, p52 top). Erik Fearn (p7 bottom, p12 top, p18 centre, p21 bottom right, p68 top & bottom, p69, top, centre &
bottom, p70 top, centre & bottom, p71 top, centre & bottom, p77 bottom). Julian Lee, Sabah Tourism (p22 bottom).
Melissa Ewot, Sabah Tourism (p9 bottom, p11 bottom, p12/13 bottom, p16 bottom, p17 top, p19, p52 bottom left, p54
bottom). Melvin Ho, Sabah Tourism (p26 top). Mountain Torq (p26 bottom, p64 top, p65 top). Sabah Parks, Sabah
Tourism (p4). Sabah Tourism (p17 bottom, p62 bottom left). Sarawak Tourism (Contents page top right, p2 bottom, p3 top
& bottom right, p7 top left & right, p9 top right, p24 top, p30 top & bottom, p31 top & bottom, p32 top, p34 top, p35
top, bottom left & right, p43 bottom, p44 top, p45 top, p46 top, p47, p48 top & bottom left, p49 top & bottom left).
Shangri-La Hotels & Resorts (p27 bottom, p28 bottom, p53 bottom, p60 top).

Cover captions and credits:
Back cover (left to right): *Rafflesia, the world's largest flower*, © Sarawak Tourist Board; *Iban tribe members at their
longhouse in Batang Ai*, © Sarawak Tourist Board; *Sipadan Island off the northeastern coast of Sabah*, © Sabah Tourism;
Gayana Eco Resort off Kota Kinabalu, © Sabah Tourism.

Front cover top (left to right): *An orchid growing in the Sabah Agricultural Park at Tenom*, © Sabah Tourism; *Sunrise
over wooden homes on stilts near the island of Maiga, Sabah*, © Shutterstcock.com/Juriah Mosin; *Mother Orang-utan
and baby*, © Shutterstock.com/Kjersti Joergensen; *Iban hunter with a blow pipe*, © Sarawak Tourist Board.
Front cover (centre): *Mount Kinabalu*, © Sabah Tourism.
Front cover (bottom): *Rhinoceros Hornbill*, © Shutterstock.com/szefei.